# THE AUTHOR'S GUIDE TO WORKING WITH BOOK BLOGGERS

BY

BARB DROZDOWICH

# COPYRIGHT

# DEDICATION

This book is dedicated to 700+ book bloggers who patiently answered my survey questions in either the first or second survey.

Thank you for sharing your thoughts.

# NOTE OF THANKS

I would like to thank you for buying one of my box sets!

I tend to focus on the technical tasks that authors and bloggers need to learn. As of this publishing I have 10 books in print and several more in various stages of completion. I'm always looking to be helpful - often creating books around subjects that I get a lot of questions on from authors and bloggers just like you.

At the end of this book is the link to get two FREE books filled with helpful hints as well as several videos delivered straight to your inbox.

On to the book - I hope you enjoy and learn lots!

# FOREWARD

I would like to welcome you to the latest edition of *The Author's Guide to Working with Book Bloggers.* This book started out based on a survey of 215 book blogger and has more recently been backed up by a second survey of 500+ book bloggers. The second survey ended this past January and although there are differences between the two sets of results, there are a lot of commonalities.

Beginner authors still struggle to understand the world of book bloggers and I feel that there is still the need to help authors walk confidently into the blogger's world.

I hope this book helps authors in their understanding of the blogging world!

# INTRODUCTION

I'M BARB Drozdowich and I blog at Sugarbeat's Books. I started my book blog in 2010 and I had no idea about the world I was about to enter.

I am a lifelong, voracious reader, one of those people who always has a book at my side. I'm also one of those people who stays up late reading, well past bedtime, because I have become caught up in a magical world and I can't bear to leave it.

I'm the daughter of an English teacher who always encouraged reading. I don't know how many books I have read so far, but it likely numbers in the thousands. Although I have gone though phases in my reading, I have always come back to romance. A tear-worthy historical romance allows the little Cinderella inside of me to live in a fantasy world for a few hours and dance with a handsome Duke at a ball.

Several years ago, I reached a point in my life where I needed an intellectual challenge. Not only that, I needed to be able to express my thoughts about the books I was reading. A friend suggested the idea of starting a book blog. I enlisted the aid of a student to put a blog together for me and I set off on a wonderful journey. For the most part, I didn't have an ever-loving clue what I was doing, and I certainly didn't think anyone would read what I had to say. I just needed this outlet, this challenge.

Once my new blog was up and running, I started posting reviews on books I had read—books from my shelves and books I found at the library. I then headed off, virtually, to find others like me—those who wanted to express their love of books on their blogs. I also needed to find other blogs to read and learn from. And find them, I did. They were everywhere! There were so many people who loved books as much as I did. Over the past few years, I have met book lovers from all over the world. I have also found so many exciting authors and been truly overwhelmed with books to read.

Because of conversations with some fellow book bloggers, I decided to conduct a survey. There are several reasons for this survey, including:

- I wanted to learn more about my fellow book bloggers.
- I wanted to see if others were experiencing the same communication-type issues between bloggers and authors that I was.

I posted a survey focused at book bloggers on my blog and advertised it on Facebook and Twitter. To my amazement, I heard from 215 book bloggers in my survey. As far as I can determine, this is the largest survey of book bloggers done to date.

Overall, did the answers surprise me? Not really. What I found was that bloggers were seeing the same things I did. I wrote the first edition of this book based on the results of the survey. I wanted to use those results to teach authors how to work in a more productive fashion with book bloggers. The first edition of this book was popular and well received. Authors commented on how helpful they found this book.

Time has passed since the original survey but what I'm seeing is that many authors still don't know how to utilize book bloggers to help promote their books. This seems to mostly be a function of how new an author is to publishing. Like any new endeavor, there is a learning curve.

The primary reason for writing the original version of this book, as well as this second edition, is to be instructional. Ultimately I want to help authors promote their books and understand how to utilize book bloggers as a free method of spreading the word about their books. I'd like to give authors as much information as I can so they aren't walking into the world of book bloggers blind.

Authors are really good at putting words together and creating magical worlds that readers lose themselves in. The promotion of these books, however, is often not their forte.

If there is one thing I hope to impress upon authors, it's that book bloggers LOVE authors. Without authors' wonderful stories, our worlds would be empty. You are our Rock Stars! We want to help you spread the word about your books to our friends and readers. If we are treated well, we will work tirelessly talking about how great your books are!

It is my intention that this book has something for everyone. For those authors who are just starting out, I hope this book can serve as an overview to the world of book promotion on book blogs. Teach you the language and help you "walk" into the world of book blogs confidently.

For those authors who have been publishing for a while, I hope this book can serve as an overview to topics you are likely familiar with, but perhaps present the information in a different way. Give you some things to think about.

It is my hope, of course, that now that you have a copy of this book, you will read it from beginning to end, but if you must, cherry pick. I'm of the mindset that we can all learn something new.

# CHAPTER ONE
# THE BOOK BLOGGERS

THE BOOK BLOGGER is a relatively new animal on the Internet. It seems like just a few years ago a website was something a highly-trained professional created at a huge cost. I know the first website I contracted came at a high price! The last few years have seen a huge change in technology, and with the advent of Wordpress and Blogger, a website is either free or well within the means of the average person.

Blogs, or weblogs as they were first called, began as an online journal or diary, often a way of allowing families to keep up to date with one another. The technology geeks were the first to embrace the idea of blogs, and technology blogs were born. These early bloggers made millions of dollars and wrote books about it. They paved the way for the rest of us, not so technologically advanced, to find a voice for our passions. Over the space of just a few years, the number and variety of blogs has simply exploded. Suddenly everyone has the ability to share their thoughts on their favorite topic with the whole world. My favorite topic is books, so my blog is referred to as a book blog.

When I was writing this book, I decided to ask Google: "How many blogs exist in 2014?" The first search result was the Wikipedia page for Blogs. The stats cited on that page stated that there are 247.8 million blogs on either Tumblr or Wordpress. Wikipedia stated that Blogger is considered to be the more popular platform for blogging but since Blogger doesn't offer any statistics, we can only guess how many blogs are active on Blogger. Think about it. That's a lot of people expressing their thoughts on the subject that interests them!

Blogs reflect the taste of their owners, and book blogs, like other blogs, can vary in focus. Many readers will read a wide variety of genres, and as a result, their blogs will comment on the varied genres they read. Some blogs, like mine, are narrower in focus. Since I read romance, the only books featured on my blog are romance of one description or another.

It should be noted that the audience of a blog will share the taste of the blogger to one extent or another. Let's take my blog as an example: I blog about romance novels. Most of the people who read my blog share my taste in reading. They certainly don't visit my blog looking for my thoughts on horror novels! A blogger who reads a variety of genres will either have an audience that also enjoys a variety of genres or an audience that picks and chooses which book promos to read and which to ignore.

Although I'll bring this subject up again in this book, keep in mind that when choosing a book blogger to help you promote your book, you will want to choose one who enjoys reading what you write. That might be an obvious point to some, but after more than four years as a book blogger, I can assure you that many authors will approach any book blogger, regardless of the blogger's preference in reading. There is no point trying to get a book blogger to read your book if they don't enjoy the genre you write and if their blog doesn't have an audience that might want to buy your book. That's just a waste of your time.

## Who are book bloggers?

The only thing we all have in common is that we love books; we love books so much that we have created blogs to express our thoughts about the books we read. Book bloggers also have access to a computer. Other than that, they can be male or female, they can vary in age, be quite computer literate, or just barely holding their own as far as technology is concerned. They may be teenagers, sharing their love of Young Adult (YA) as they conquer their high school classes; they may be stay-at-home moms spending their free time sharing their thoughts on their favorite books as an escape from the kids. They may be budding authors using a book blog as a way to experiment with their writing. A book blogger may be a parent/child duo, with the parent encouraging the child to read more. They may be newly retired, looking for a mental challenge and a way to share their lifelong love of books.

Book blogging is usually a hobby; it is something that is done in a blogger's spare time. If book bloggers make money from ads on their blogs, it generally isn't much. There are a few exceptions, of course, but in general, book blogging and reviewing books is something book bloggers do for no pay.

Many book bloggers started blogging to simply share their thoughts with other book lovers. Take a look at this selection of the answers I received when I asked the question, "Why did you start book blogging?"

- "Because I wanted to be able to share great books with other readers."
- "I started reading book blogs after joining GoodReads. I already had other blogs and felt like book blogging was something fun I could also do. I have an eclectic taste in books, and I wanted to share that beyond GoodReads."
- "I am very supportive of many changes taking place in the book industry. I am particularly supportive of e-books and talented Indie and small press authors and LOVE helping spread the word about their books. I also personally enjoy discovering 'new to me' authors who can help support my book addiction."
- "I love to read. This was a way to share what I like and to find new books and authors to read."
- "To talk with other book lovers, and to have a creative outlet online."
- "I wanted someone to discuss books with and there aren't any book clubs in my area."
- "To have a place to talk about books, to be a part of a community."
- "I love reading and none of my friends understand, so I decided to join a community that not only understands, but embraces my nerdiness."
- "To encourage my students, to share my love of books."
- "I started my blog as a place to put my writing, but when I discovered book blogs I thought, 'I have to be a part of this.'"
- "As a hobby/just for fun."
- Nothing is better than finding "that" book. The one that rings your bell. I like helping people find it!"
- "I wanted an outlet to discuss YA literature—not many people in my real life read the same genre/category as I do or even as voraciously. Online seemed the logical place to go to find other readers like me."
- "To have a place to put my thoughts about the books I read, to meet other people who love reading as much as I do, and to be able to create something to be proud of."
- "I read a lot. I started writing reviews because I know

authors like them. I started posting them to help other readers find great books."

- • "I wanted to share my opinions on books for others to see. Plus, there aren't many people I know in my school who read the same books I do, so it makes it hard to gush."

- • "To share my love of books with the world."

- • "I wanted a way to keep myself writing at least something down. That way I might not get writer's block as often for my writing projects. It is also a way for me to discuss my love for books and find new books that are out there."

- • "Because I wanted to find new readers like me who are big romance fans to discuss books with and share this big passion of mine!"

- • "To create a space where my kids and I give our opinions about children's books—we don't always agree!"

Since I received 215 responses to my original survey, you can well imagine there were many answers to this question. I've listed my favorite ones above.

The answer from the list that I liked the most was: "To share my love of books with the world." This topic will come up over and over again in this book. Book selling is a relationship-based activity. So many studies have been done that tell us people buy books based on a suggestion from a friend or a trusted source. That "friend" may now be half a world away.

When I post a review or other feature on my blog, it is open to be read by anyone, no matter what country they live in. Book blogging takes the relationship-selling model and blows it up in terms of reach. The audience doesn't even need to speak the same language with many blogs. The next time you visit a blog, see if the blog has the ability to be translated to a different language. That functionality is more common than you think.

In conclusion, the only generalization that can be made is that book bloggers love books. This, of course infers that all book bloggers are unique, just like all humans are unique. They can't really be generalized. Not only do they differ in their reading tastes, they will differ in the way they run their blogs. They have things they accept, and things they don't accept, things they like and things they don't like.

**Now that we know what book bloggers are, how do we find them?**

Do you do a Google search using the search terms "book + blogger" and the genre you write in? That might work, but there are existing databases that are somewhat accurate to one extent or another that can be used as a good starting point.

http://bookbloggerlist.com
http://www.theindieview.com/indie-reviewers/

Both of these sites list book bloggers either by genre or alphabetically. There may be a short write-up about each blog to give you an idea if it is a good match for you. This will allow you to quickly whittle down a large list of book bloggers into a manageable size that can be investigated further. For the sake of clarity, The Book Blogger List, the first one I listed above, is my site. It was started about two years ago and has about 2000 listings.

Why not ask a friend? If you belong to a critique group or have author friends, they probably have had some contact with book bloggers. Talk to them. Who do they know? Who are their favorite bloggers?

Have your author friends toured their books with a blog tour company? Follow their tour and look at where they visit. Drop by the site of some of the blog tour companies, and look at their sidebars. Many list the blogs that are tour hosts. Work your way through this list and visit some blogs.

I'm sure you're starting to realize that finding bloggers to be friends of yours may be viewed as a goose chase. You find yourself a starting point—let's say a book blogger an author friend of yours suggested. Go to his blog and look around. Look at who comments on his posts and visit some of their blogs. Look at the sidebars of book blogs. Who is listed in their blogrolls? Many book bloggers love badges! They post the badges of their friends on their sidebars. Visit their friends. We want you to; that's one of the reasons we advertise who they are!

I do, however, encourage you to not "reinvent the wheel" as the saying goes. There are great starting points to use in your search—like my Book Blogger List. Make use of them. Allow them to make your search easier.

However you find them, create a list of bloggers who read the genres you write, and seem like people you would like to know, to be friends with. How do you make friends in the bloggy world? You say "Hi, my name is . . . " just like in the real world. We'll talk more about this in Chapter 4.

As we come to the end of this chapter, you have learned a bit about what book bloggers are and some information on where to find some. You'll want to make use of this source of free promotions, but I find many authors are puzzled by the terminology. You don't want to have the newbie stamp on your forehead when you start asking for promotions. Over the next few chapters, I will define and describe the various types of promotions available via book bloggers. I hope you learn something new as you work your way though the next few chapters and are able to use this new knowledge in the promotion of your book.

# CHAPTER TWO

# The Book Blogger Platform

THERE IS MUCH talk about what an Author Platform is, but not much talk about what a Book Blogger Platform is. However, I am often asked by authors, "How do I find good blog to promote my book?" Obviously, this is the question that prompted the creation of The Book Blogger List, but I think the key word in this question is the word "good." In other words, how can an author determine if the book blogger they choose to read or feature his book has anyone reading what he writes ? Let's see if we can flesh out this topic.

If you want book bloggers to promote your book, they must have some sort of an audience to promote it to. As nice as it is to visit with bloggy friends and have a virtual chat, when promoting a book, you want to get as much bang for your buck as you can. Just as authors should be hooked into various social media, so should bloggers if they are going to attract a large audience and therefore promote your book to as many people as possible.

## What do you look for when searching for a blogger to promote your book?

It is obvious to state that a book blogger needs a blog, but have you actually looked at the blogs you have run across? How do you determine the blogs that have a larger audience?

Many people assume that you determine the popularity of a blog by the number of comments left on each post. That isn't necessarily true. Are there blogs out there that get many comments? Yes. There are also blogs that get high traffic numbers and have few comments. So comments aren't necessarily an indication of traffic.

Some time ago, most book bloggers had a "Google Friend Connect" widget on their sidebar that clearly indicated how many "friends" they had. Access to the widget has been restricted to Blogger blogs; it no longer works on Wordpress (or other platform) blogs. When I first started blogging, I was in awe of how many blogs had such high numbers of "friends." I quickly discovered, however, how easy it is to artificially inflate those numbers. So, is a high number of "friends" on Google Friend Connect an indication of a popular blog? Maybe, but not necessarily.

There are several other widgets that bloggers use that may or may not be helpful. Many will use a Feedburner or Jetpack widget that indicates the number of subscribers. In fact, many book bloggers will actually post their stats on their blogs, as they are trying to attract advertising dollars.

What you are trying to determine is how many hits you will get if you have something posted to their blogs. The most straightforward way to determine this is to ask. Many book bloggers will tell you. One thing I want you to keep in mind is there is more to be concerned with than just hits on a blog. It's more complex than that.

A quick and dirty way to evaluate a blog is to check it out on Alexa (a service that ranks websites). I have an Alexa toolbar on my browser so I can see the Alexa ranking of every site I visit. Is determining the Alexa for a site the answer to all your questions? No, but it's easy to take a quick look. There are also times when a blog simply doesn't have an Alexa ranking. I won't even pretend to understand why that is, but to me, it is a point of concern. When you look at an Alexa ranking, the closer the number is to 1, the better the site is. The Google home page has an Alexa ranking of 1. Most popular book blogs will have an Alexa ranking somewhere between 250,000 to 600,000. Since I'm quite certain that more than actual hits are involved in making up an Alexa ranking, there are valid reasons for blogs ranking higher or lower than this range.

Again, is the Alexa ranking the end of the story? I don't think so. Many think Klout is a good measure of the influence of a blogger. Again, it may tell part of the story, but not the whole story.

The total reach of a book blogger is made up of more than just her blog reach. You must look at the whole package of her social media.

Back to what makes up the book blogger platform. Other than the blog, book bloggers should have a minimum of a healthy Twitter and Facebook following. Look at their Twitter accounts and see if they are active on Twitter—do they do nothing but spam links, or are they interacting? The same on Facebook. Do they just post their feeds to their Facebook page, or are they interacting? Essentially, are they chatting about books? Will they chat about YOUR book?

Do you write YA? Are the bloggers active on the social media sites frequented by the younger readers? Are they active on Instagram and others?

I have been doing a lot of reading on Google+ lately and I'm becoming increasingly convinced that everyone needs a presence on Google+. Although there is a lot of disagreement about its importance, it is gaining in popularity and I think you'll be hearing more and more about Google+ in the near future (especially if Facebook keeps changing in the direction that it is).

Book bloggers are often active on Pinterest. I love Pinterest—I can spend hours on Pinterest! From beautiful landscape pictures to eye-catching book covers, Pinterest has something for everyone. There is nothing like having your book cover posted on someone's Pin board for everyone to see—especially if it has the comment "Great book" or "Excellent Read." Goodreads and Shelfari are also popular with book bloggers, with some preferring one over the other. Is the book blogger active on Amazon? Goodreads and Amazon are often secondary places where reviews can be posted and book bloggers often link to these pages. Many of Amazon's top reviewers are also book bloggers. If they are an Amazon Top Reviewer or an Amazon Vine member, they are proud of this and often advertise it on their blog. Many book bloggers are part of tribes on Triberr. If you are not familiar with Triberr, it is a site that you can belong to as part of a tribe of like-minded individuals. It is called a "Reach Multiplier." This site gives tribe members the ability to tweet and otherwise promote each other's blog posts. Triberr can expand the reach of the blogger by huge proportions. The tweets are sent out in a measured separation determined by the blogger—often set at 40 minutes. Tribes that are huge can have tweets appearing days after the original post. This, of course, means you could have visitors to your feature days after it originally went up. Because of this and as a general practice, you should subscribe to comments on the blog you are being featured on so you can be notified when a new comment appears. We'll talk more about this in other chapters.Lastly, look at a Google search. Where do the blogger's posts end up? Just choose a post that has been around for a bit and Google the author or the name of the book or the title of the post. Ideally, you want a blogger whose posts are popular enough to rank fairly high in a search for future reference. Although you want a big promotion for your book, you also want longevity. You want a post that will be found days or even months later when someone is doing a related Google search. Essentially, this will allow you to amass a body of work that is easily found on Google! However, before you jump into the Book Blogging world to get some attention paid to your book, we need to talk a bit about book marketing.

# CHAPTER THREE
# BOOK MARKETING 101

I'VE BEEN WORKING in the world of books and authors for several years. Everyone seems to have an opinion about how best to promote or market your book. Wearing my "book blogger" hat, I've been sitting back and watching what works for me as a consumer, as a buyer of books, for several years now. I've come to the conclusion that throwing money at someone doesn't sell books; whether that person is a PR representative, a tour company, or an agent, a relationship with the author is what sells books. Although there is no "magic bullet" that applies to every book, there are some generalizations that can be made. Let's explore this further.

As we all know, the world of publishing is changing rapidly. With the advent of independent publishing, anyone can write a story and be a published author. The big publishing houses no longer control the right to be "published." This has resulted in a huge influx of "published authors." People can take it upon themselves to publish their own book. In an article dated July 28, 2014, Publisher's Weekly quotes a number of interesting facts. Did you know self-published books represent 31% of all e-book sales on Amazon's Kindle Store? In fact, Indie authors are earning nearly 40% of the e-book dollars going to authors.

In another article in Publisher's Weekly dated Nov 10, 2014, they quote information from Bowker, the official U.S. ISBN agency by saying that ISBNs associated with self-published books has climbed 437% between 2008 and 2013. They also note that that increase doesn't include books that did not get their ISBN from Bowker, were published without an ISBN, or acquired their ISBN from Amazon or other sources. Huge number!

Every publication, it seems, will spout numbers of how many books are self-published, what the increase is each year, or over a span of years. Suffice it to say that independent publishing is increasing, and the publishing world, overall, is in flux.

The publishing world is changing in more ways than who gets to be published. The world of book promotions is changing as well. The consumer is determining who will be a best-selling author. The consumer in the book world is a hard sell. Marketing practices that work well to sell shoes or hamburgers don't work well with books. Book sales are more personal. They are sold on word of mouth. They are sold on recommendation by a friend. What do you say to someone reading a book? "Is it any good?" "What do you think?" If you're a fan of the author, you might ask, "Is it as good as the rest of their books?" It is often said that selling books is a relationship business.

Many studies have been done to determine why people buy books. When readers are asked what encourages them to buy/choose a book, every study has three top reasons. They may change in order of importance, but they are always the same. People list the following as a reason to buy a book:

- History with the author
- Cover art
- Recommendation from a friend, family member, or other trusted source

Let's talk about each of these reasons.

- History with the author is a huge motivating factor for me as well as others. Once I discover an author I love, I then work my way through their backlist. If I like one of the books they have written, I will probably like the rest. To insert a plug for e-books here, it's wonderful that authors are putting their older backlist books up as e-books. Talk about instant gratification. I can finish one book and be shopping on my Nook in minutes!

- Cover art is very influential. Regardless of the genre, the cover speaks to readers. It lets them know if this book is their genre, and the assumption is that it gives them a glimpse into the story. I'm very attracted to the cover art of the genre I read. I love wandering (virtually or in person) along bookstore aisles looking for a cover that speaks to me.

- I know when I finish a particularly good book, I just want to tell someone; I just want someone else to enjoy what I have just enjoyed! Hence, the blog, of course, but in real life, also. I'm not a keeper of books. Once I have finished with a book, I give it away, or take it to a used bookstore to get credit to buy more books. If I take it to the used book store, I always hope someone else will find it and love it as much as I did!

I am, at heart, a pretty shy person. I don't chat easily with strangers, but I will almost always ask them about what they're reading. Do they like the book? Have they read other books by that author? Would they recommend the book they are reading? I do the same with friends and family members. Few of my family members read the same genres I do, but I'm always curious about what they like (or don't like), what they are reading. Being in the blogging world, I'm constantly exposed to all sorts of books and people's thoughts about these books. There's nothing I like more than to be able to recommend a book to other readers and have them come back and tell me they loved it!

With this new electronic age of publishing comes the massive proliferation of book bloggers. The affordability of blogs allows readers to have their own forum to express their thoughts about books. One article I read described book bloggers as "the publisher's new slush pile". Author and Social Media Guru, Anne R Allen, describes book bloggers as the New Gatekeepers. (The New Gatekeepers: How to Query a Book Review Blogger—an Interview with Danielle Smith posted On Anne R. Allen's blog at url: http://annerallen.com/2011/11/new-gatekeepers-how-to-query-book.html)

People like me who have book blogs, have thousands of friends and followers we can share our recommendations with. The recommendation that was once in person, between friends or family members, is now international. I have blogs that I read on a regular basis written by people in Australia, Germany, England, India, and the Philippines, to name just a few countries. The world of recommendation is huge! I can post a review of a book, and within seconds, someone on the other side of the world can read my thoughts and maybe purchase a copy of this book. Book clubs that were once limited to in-person activities, where readers gather at a local library, coffee shop, or someone's home, now are online. They are in chat rooms, they are on Spreecast, they are on Goodreads. Many of the members will never meet in person; in fact, they often don't live in the same country, let alone within easy driving distance. I find it fascinating to hear what people from vastly different cultures think about certain books.

You can see that book blogs and the Internet have taken the concept of "recommendation by a friend" and blown it up to huge proportions! The formation of relationships is no longer a simple in-person activity; it is a huge international activity.

Since book selling is seen as a relationship-based activity, how does an author who lives in Washington State build that relationship with a fan who lives in England or Australia? That fan certainly won't be coming to book signings at the local bookstore! And the author can't be expected to travel to all the countries his fans live in. This is where blogs, both author blogs and book blogs, shine. Although not the focus of this book, author blogs are an essential part of the author's platform. They help the reader, especially the reader from a different country, form a relationship with the author.

Book blogs not only allow a reader to talk about books and their thoughts about them; in many cases, they provide a platform for an author to interact with readers without leaving her house. In fact, they provide a venue for authors to interact with readers without spending a dime! Book bloggers love books and love promoting authors. Frankly, without authors, my world and the world of other book bloggers/book lovers would be pretty empty.

If we use the example of my book blog, I have seven days a week to share my thoughts about books. I have a venue and an audience, and if I chose, I could post multiple times a day. I have a day job and my blog, like many book blogs, is a hobby. I can't read and review seven books a week. I simply don't have enough free time! How do I fill these seven days? I post other types of features, usually only one a day. We'll get into the various different types of promotions in other chapters.

# CHAPTER FOUR
## ETIQUETTE OF THE BLOGOSPHERE

ALTHOUGH THIS book initially started based on a survey of book bloggers, much of the information I learned from the survey is still true. In fact, it has been reinforced by a second survey carried out more recently. Many concerns were raised in both surveys regarding etiquette—manners, if you will. As I'm sure many of you are aware, there are still many examples of bad behavior on social media and much improvement needed with respect to etiquette!

I think there is something about social media that allows people to forget their manners. Things that people certainly wouldn't do or say in person, they have no problem doing online. Let's take a few moments and talk about manners.

We'll move through a number of broad topics while keeping in mind two key points:

1. All Book Bloggers are unique. They all have preferences, not only in their reading selections but also in the way in which they operate their blog. The vast majority of them have a "review policy." A review policy is where book bloggers state what they read (and what they don't read), what they post to their blog, and how they want to be queried.

2. Book Bloggers, like the rest of society, are more likely to do a favor for a friend that they wouldn't do for a stranger. Because of this, it is in your best interest to make friends with some book bloggers! In previous chapters we discussed how to find some book blogs that suit the genre you write in. I suggested you visit a few and go on a "goose chase" to find some bloggers who are potential friends.

How do you make friends in the blogosphere? The same way you do in Kindergarten. Think back: "Hi, my name is Barb. Will you be my friend?" Okay, maybe we're a little more sophisticated now. Think about the last party, or the last conference you went to. You likely introduced yourself to people you didn't know. I find the best way to introduce myself to someone new is to offer a compliment as a conversation starter. "Hi, my name is Barb. I love your scarf! Where did you get it?"

The same method works in the online world. Let's go back to the example of a blog you are visiting. Have a look around; actually read what the blogger has written. Leave a comment that reflects the fact that you're trying to be friendly. "Hi, my name is Barb and this is my first visit to your blog. I really enjoyed reading your review of Book XYZ. Looks like I'm heading to the bookstore to pick up a copy." When you leave the comment, make sure you leave your e-mail address and your blog URL (usually required on most comment systems). You'll notice this comment is friendly without being self-promotional. Probably one of the worst things you can do is to leave the following comment: "Hi, my name is Barb and this is my first visit here. I enjoyed your review of Book XYZ and I must tell you I have written a similar, yet better story, which you really must review. I'm e-mailing you a copy and will expect a glowing review shortly."

You think I exaggerate? Not really! I can't count the number of times I have had people leave similar comments on my blog. I have received many unsolicited books over the years. Not only is it rude, but sending unsolicited books is a recipe for piracy. I know I'm honest, but how does the author know I won't upload the book to a piracy site?

Back to making book blogger friends: Leaving comments along with the ability to contact you back will allow bloggers to visit your world. Just like you dropped by to say hi, they might drop by to say hi on your blog, too. I must admit, it often takes leaving a few comments for bloggers to get curious and follow your links to visit you. I suggest you make a list of bloggers you are interested in befriending and drop by once a week to say hi. It doesn't need to be time consuming—choose five to visit each morning while you are having your first cup of coffee. Frankly, following links has led me to some of my best author friends. I get curious and go visiting. When I arrive at their blog, I see the cover of a book that seems right for me. I ask questions and I find a new friend—and a new book to read.

If you take one thing away from this chapter, I hope it will be not to self-promote when trying to make friends. Picture yourself at a party where you don't know anyone. Do you walk from person to person, handing out books, saying "Read my book; call me"? Of course you don't. Interaction on social media should reflect the real world.

Let's move on to Facebook and Twitter. These social medias are often viewed as very different. Yes, there are some differences between them, but they are both vehicles of communication. Twitter is the place for short communications and Facebook is the place for longer and more varied communications. They are both places where you can expand your brand, talk about things that are important to you, and share interesting or funny things. The people who follow you or like you are part of your growing community—your group of friends who will help you get the news out about your book.

Show some respect for the blogger's time and energy. It is NOT all right to ask someone to review your book just because she has followed you on Twitter. I find that it's not unusual to get some version of: "Hi! I'd like to send you a free e-copy of my new book IMPISH for Kindle or Kindle app—no strings attached. If interested, shoot me a DM!" My friend Rachel Thompson has a great blog post about this: (http://badredheadmedia.com/2012/10/24/7-ways-youre-unintentionally-spamming-people/). As a quick heads up, auto DMs are considered a faux pas in today's world of social media. Asking everyone to read your book because they follow you on Twitter or Facebook is the equivalent of attending a party where you don't know anyone, and going from person to person handing out business cards and asking them to read your book. Think about it . . . do you really think you would have a lot of luck? Then don't try it on social media!

I'm sure you would never do any of the above to convince bloggers to read your book! I'm also sure that you think I'm exaggerating. Sadly, I'm not. It's a daily occurrence in my world.

Although there are literally thousands of book bloggers, the book blogging world is a small one. We talk. Book blogging is a social activity. Do we all talk to one another? No. But just as gossip flies like wildfire in the real world, gossip flies on social media at warp speed. Any example of bad behavior is passed around quickly. Don't be the next example of "what not to do" that is passed around Twitter.

# CHAPTER FIVE
# REVIEW ETIQUETTE

PUBLISHING A BOOK used to be controlled by publishers and by and large the big publishing houses controlled their authors' behavior. Periodically there was someone who went off on a tangent, but it was a fairly unusual occurrence. We now have the ability for anyone to write a book and have it published. This is a good thing . . . and a bad thing.

Authors can't just tell stories any longer. They have to have so many more skills than they used to have. I suppose authors were always involved in promoting their own books to some extent, but these days, it involves the use of technology. We expect authors to maintain a blog and operate multiple social media accounts, and that is on top of writing, likely working a full-time job and being part of a family! So many things to learn. So many things to juggle.

The pressure of being a published author in today's world is great. Combine that with the fact that most authors try to do everything themselves as they simply don't have the budget to hire help. In many cases an author doesn't have anyone in her immediate surroundings to serve as a sounding board.

We have all seen the results of poorly thought out words on the part of the author and the book blogger. Generally it is in response to a review of an author's book. Those all important reviews! The subject of "Authors behaving badly" or "Book bloggers behaving badly" seems to have become a normal occurrence on the social media streams. What was once an unusual thing seems to be becoming a regular event.

This past fall I was at a writing conference and one of the workshops I attended was on reviews. The presenter, Sarah Wendell from Smart Bitches, Trashy Books (http://smartbitchestrashybooks.com/) said an interesting thing. She said the reviews authors get BEFORE their books are published are for them. Those would be the ones from their publishing house, their editor, their beta readers and perhaps their critique group. All the reviews AFTER the book is published are for readers.

My immediate response to that comment was NO! Then I thought about it. And I thought about it. And I decided that she is absolutely correct. The critical reviews that help an author determine whether a book is ready to publish are the ones for the author. They should be based on dispassionate criteria. How good is the storytelling . . . how good is the editing, etc.

Once the book is released to the world by being published, it will be subjected to readers' reactions. There are many readers in the world. Not all of them subscribe to the old adage of, "If you can't say something nice, say nothing at all." Some readers go out of their way to be hurtful. If they have spent their hard-earned money on a book and it didn't meet their expectations, they may lash out. In fact, some book bloggers attract a really large audience by being snarky. Let's face it—it's like watching a train wreck. You can't turn away. Who are they going to skewer next?

## Does a bad review of your book hurt? YES! Absolutely!

Let's divide bad reviews into two types—just plain mean, and a detailed critique of what the reader finds wrong with the book.

Reviews that are mean—by that I mean the review where the book obviously didn't meet the expectations of the reader, and she is lashing out. Maybe she bought your book thinking it was something it wasn't and she is taking her anger out on you . . . and sadly, the whole world can read about it because she posted that review to Amazon.

The vast majority of these reviews should be ignored. You'll notice I said the vast majority. If you start to see some commonalities you might have some problems that need to be fixed. For example, if quite a few people comment that the story ends abruptly at the end of chapter 6, but you actually have 25 chapters in your book, maybe there is something wrong with the file you uploaded to the various retailers. If quite a few people comment on feeling misled about what the story was about, perhaps you need to look at your book blurb and other promotional material and see if any changes need to be made.

Sadly, just like in other areas of society, there will be people who choose to be mean and rude. You see it at the grocery store, Walmart—everywhere in normal life. Reviews of books are no different. The key point is to not take reviews like this personally and certainly don't respond to them.

Reviews that are a detailed critique of what the reader finds wrong with the book can serve as a valuable tool. Although authors go through the process of beta readers, editing, proofreading, and professional formatting, there are things that are not caught. A review that details errors the reader found while reading your book can be a valuable resource—and can help you make corrections quickly, and a new version of your book can be uploaded to the retailers. Remember, readers come from all walks of life and bring all sorts of experience to their reading. They can be a valuable resource.

Authors seem to strive for all positive reviews. This is an unrealistic expectation. Not everyone is going to love your book! What makes a book a great read to one person makes it horrible to another. All you have to do is read the reviews on some of history's most treasured books to find people who didn't like them. The key point in this is that readers can tell the difference between a helpful review and a non-helpful review.

Let's give some examples. If I were to read a review that tells me the reader found the book to be littered with grammatical errors that should have been caught before publishing, I would give that book a wide berth. Nothing drives me battier than grammatical errors while I'm trying to enjoy a story. If a review of a book criticized the time period that the story was set in—let's say the reader hated the story because it was set in Regency England and he felt this was the most depressing time period in England's history—that comment would likely have me reaching for my wallet, as I LOVE stories set in Regency England. The example Sarah gave in the workshop I attended was comments about too much sex in a book. The amount of sex in a book that one person finds offensive has another person reaching for her wallet.

Do you ever look at a book that has nothing but 5-star reviews and wonder if the author bought those reviews? Very few books elicit only a flawless response from readers. Since all readers are different, hopefully they will all have a different response to your book, resulting in a variety of ratings. As an artist, you want to evoke a response from your readers. I think the worst response a reader can have is, "Well, that was a book." Isn't it better for a reader to get to the end of your story and be excited about sharing your book with someone else? Either excited about how great it is, or how bad they felt it was.

## Reader reviews do not ruin careers.

This is a comment I hear all the time—"bad reviews will ruin an author's career." Before we continue, let's be clear—a whole bunch of bad reviews about editing errors is a concern that need to be addressed, but a whole bunch of "bad" reviews of your horror novel because it scared the stuffing out of your readers is a good thing. People will buy a book to see if it is really "that bad" or really "that scary." Readers know their tastes. They know what they will like and not like. A horror novel that scares the stuffing out of some is just the ticket to others.

Haven't you picked up a book based on a "bad" review only to wonder if the reviewer read the same book as you just did?

## How to respond to negative reviews

We know from recent history that it is not acceptable to stalk someone, go to her house and try to change her mind about your book, or travel across country and break a wine bottle over her head resulting in a hospital stay and stitches, or mail someone dog poo. Sadly, all these things have happened. You don't want to be the next "author behaving badly." You have two choices in your response to a review.

1. You can politely thank the reader for reading your book.
2. You can do nothing.

In a very small number of situations it is possible to contact a reviewer who left a critical review to get him to send you a list of things he felt needed to be changed –grammatical errors, for example. I know an author who received a review criticizing the grammar of some French phrases in her novel. She contacted the reviewer and got a list of errors the reviewer felt needed to be changed. This situation is rare. Many readers would refuse to send you a list—they just want to be angry about your errors, not be helpful.

There are people whom we refer to as "Trolls." Just like the mythical creatures, Trolls live to create havoc. Trolls often leave mean reviews. Responding to trolls is exactly what they want. They are looking for a response they can pounce on. And pounce they will and make sure everyone knows how bad your book is, and how unkind you were to respond. Words will be taken out of context and you will end up the loser. Therefore, don't respond, don't get your friends to respond and don't encourage your fans on social media to defend you. It will only end badly.

Social Media has taken the world and made it very small. Along with that, anything you post on any social media, including your blog, is "out there" for everyone to see and it isn't going away. Tweets are re-tweeted, Facebook messages are shared and shared again, and blog posts can stay cached on Google for a really long time.

There is a course at my local high school that is the modern-day equivalent of what would have been called "Health" when I was in school. Amongst other things they teach in this course, they talk about the long-term implications of posting something to social media. How that drunken picture of you and your friends can get you turned down by a university that you want to attend. How that Twitter chat with your friends can get you fired from your job.

I think that course should be taught to those of us too old to still be in high school. Although a slew of bad reviews by Trolls won't ruin your career, your response to them may make book bloggers think twice about agreeing to feature your book. As you will find out from this book, book bloggers are a great source of free promotions. We talk, however. And we are on social media. We often research an author before agreeing to promote her book. If you have had a virtual screaming match with a reader, how do we know you won't do the same with us? If you have sent your fans to respond to a review, how do we know we won't be the target of an attack?

So . . . the only response you can have to a review is: "Thank you for taking the time to read my book."

# CHAPTER SIX
# THE QUERY

LET'S RECAP. You've learned about book bloggers, who they are and where they can be found. You have, hopefully, spent some time finding some bloggers who read your genre and have started commenting and making some book blogger friends. Now you're ready to start approaching some book bloggers to see if you can get some reviews or other types of promotion.

The main point to keep in mind is that you want some attention for your book. In order to do that, you need to approach some book bloggers to see what they can do for you. This step will involve what is commonly known as "The Query." Most publishing houses and agents require a query letter when submitting a book for their consideration. If your book has been published, this should not be an unfamiliar task for you.

A few words about genre before we move on. When asking for a review of your book, you want to ensure that your book is in "friendly" hands. Why badger a blogger into reading your horror novel when they say they only read romance? Their one star review will likely start with: "Don't buy this book: it is horrible; it will scare you." Don't you want the book to be reviewed by someone who likes having a book scare them? Likewise, when you're asking for some sort of promotion, don't you want your book promoted to an audience that's likely to buy your book? If we take the example from above, why try to promote your Horror novel on a Romance site? Not many of the readers of that blog would be interested in buying your book, as they don't like scary books. Why go to the time and effort to promote your book in a place where you aren't likely to generate any sales? Make sure you're likely to get the "biggest bang for your buck," as the saying goes.

Now you have a tentative list of book bloggers whom you would like to approach to read your book. Let's start with the first book blogger on your list. Even if you have been to this blog before, you'll need to refresh your memory on the information in her Review Policy.

Read the blogger's review policy or information page carefully, noting how she wants to be approached—by e-mail or by filling out an embedded form—what kind of timeline she is currently working on, and what she will or won't accept. It's her blog—she is the queen of the castle, and she makes the rules. Just like querying a publishing house, your query will likely be deleted if you don't follow the guidelines. Keep in mind that many experienced bloggers can get hundreds of queries a month. Give them a reason NOT to delete yours.

The average book blogger cannot possibly read and review hundreds of books a month even if they have a team of reviewers, so let's talk about how to increase the odds of your book being accepted for a feature.

A quick review of what NOT to do:
- Do not send a form letter or anything resembling a form letter; bloggers can spot these a mile away, and they frequently end up in the trash bins of experienced bloggers.
- Do not send the query to 'Dear Sir/Madam" or anything resembling this; address them personally. I know I don't appreciate being addressed as "Ms Sugarbeat's Books" when it isn't difficult to determine my name from looking at my blog.
- Do not automatically attach an electronic copy of your book. Not only is it considered presumptuous; unsolicited books are in danger of being pirated.

Now that we have the big no-nos out of the way, let's focus on what to do.

I'm going to make the assumption that the book blogger doesn't have a preset form for you to fill in and has requested an e-mail to be sent. Let's create a general overview of what would be appropriate to include in your query letter.
- State "Review," "Guest Post" or "Interview Request" (or specifically what you want to ask about) in the subject of the e-mail. If you are asking for a review, please make sure the book blogger is open to reviews. Likewise, if you are requesting a guest post and the author does not host guest posts, your e-mail will likely be deleted. You really don't want to prove right off the bat that you haven't read the policy page.
- Address your note to the blogger by name. With

very few exceptions, book bloggers identify themselves on their blogs, either by name or nickname.

• You want to be fairly formal, but as I said above, there is nothing worse than "Dear Sir/Madam," or "Dear Blogger," or in my case, "Dear Sugarbeat's Books." I have a name and it's easy to find on my blog.

• In the body of the letter, reiterate what you are requesting. If your primary request is for a review, state that. You might want to offer alternatives right at the beginning of the letter. For example: "I can see you write a very busy blog and I was hoping you would have time to review my book, XX, but if not, I am certainly open to other promotional opportunities, such as guest posts, giveaways, or interviews." This gives the blogger an out. Maybe he isn't completely taken with the blurb of your book, but it fits within his genre preferences. Offering other activities allows the blogger to promote your book without actually reading and reviewing it.

• Give some details for the book. What is generally required is Title, Author (if different from the name you send the e-mail under), Publisher (state Indie if self-pubbed), Genre (specifically), Release Date, and Length. Length is often the deciding factor for some bloggers. I know personally I can't read a book over about 325 pages. I find it too overwhelming and start to lose interest. Those epic novels of 600 pages are not for me. You need to allow the blogger to make an educated decision about whether or not to review your book. Again, you don't want a review that says: "This would have been a great book if it was only 300 pages, but I found the 600 pages just too much to wade through, so I'm giving this book a 2 star because it went on and on and on. It was WAY too long." You might be saying to yourself, "That would never happen." I challenge you to look at reviews on Amazon and revise your opinion of what people are willing to complain about.

• Provide a blurb for the book and either an excerpt or a link to an excerpt. Many bloggers like to use the excerpt to get a feel for the author's writing style. This is very important to them.

• Cover Art—I, like many others, enjoy seeing the cover art. I'm quite a visual person and often make my decision whether to review or not based on the blurb and the cover.

• What formats are available for the blogger to read? All you need to do is look at a few review policies to see that many bloggers have strong opinions as to what format they choose to read. Many of us have moved to primarily reading electronic versions of books, but there is a large percentage of bloggers who will only read paper versions. If you have multiple formats available, list what you have. The other point I'll add here is that not all book bloggers live in the same country as you do. If a blogger chooses to read a paper version of your book, mailing it might be expensive. A little hint—why not gift a blogger a book from Amazon or Barnes & Noble? Not only is it likely cheaper than the mail, but it will also be a "verified" purchase when they leave a review.

• Is the book you're offering for review part of a series? If so, which book in the series? Also, if the book is part of a series, you might want to provide some information about the series itself. Many bloggers are unwilling to read books out of order. Many bloggers, myself included, are annoyed to get partially through a book only to figure out the book is in the middle of a series and that's why there are all sorts of unreferenced activities and characters. I've been known to abandon a book like that and find the first book in the series to start there. We are back to the question of do you really want to see this in a review?: "I found this book very confusing. It seemed full of insider information that I had trouble figuring out. I wouldn't recommend this book." Remember, you are familiar with the story line; we are not!

• Include several links not only to where the book is for sale (if published), but also author blog/website/social media links. Although book bloggers love to read, and have chosen to write a blog, many of them are also interested in being part of a promotion team. I personally always look at an author's blog as well as her Twitter/Facebook streams. Not only does it give me a feel for an author's writing, it also gives me an idea of whether the author is invested in promoting the book and the bloggers who promote them. Why would I go to the trouble of promoting a book if the author isn't going to reciprocate? We'll talk some more in other chapters about the author's responsibility for blog dates. There are many reasons for including the above links, but suffice it to say it could be a deal breaker. Another point to add here is that bloggers will re-search authors to determine their behavior. Too many bloggers have been either attacked or at the very least put in the position of having to defend their thoughts to an aggressive author. With limited reading hours, and almost unlimited books, we can afford to be choosy.

• State a possible date range that you are interested in visiting the blog. If you are trying to promote a new release and are hoping for a review, keep in mind many bloggers book dates on their blogs months in advance. If your publication date is four weeks away and you really want something to coin-cide with your publication date, please be up front about that. Each blogger will schedule his blog differently, and may be able to adjust for requested dates.

• In closing, please include your name (and pen name, if different than your real name), position (if other than the author), and some contact information.

You can see how tempting it is to put all the information in a form letter and just mass mail it. Book bloggers can spot a form letter a mile away. Since most of us receive so many queries each week, we have to have some way of narrowing the field. Let's face it, we're like kids in a candy store. Books are our candy and there are only so many reading hours available to us. At the time of the printing of this book, I gener-ally receive about 200-300 queries a month.

You would think it's a no-brainer to follow the rules that book bloggers create when sending them a query. It's just like submitting your book to a publishing house. You need to submit a query that con-forms to the rules or yours hits the trash can.

In reality, book bloggers often don't get what they require to make an informed decision. You are asking someone to take the time to do something so you can make money. I'm quite certain the vast majority of queries I get that are vague are due to the author's lack of knowl-edge. That's why I'm writing this book: I'm hoping to fill in some of these fuzzy areas.

# Chapter Seven
# The Review

THE MUCH sought-after review consumes a lot of an author's energies. It is seen as the key to the kingdom by many. I will admit that reviews are a necessary thing on Amazon and other purchasing sites these days; people have the ability everywhere to state their view on a product, and many do. As the buying public, we can consult these reviews to determine if we want to buy a product. How much credence we give them is a personal choice.

I'm sure you've noticed that reviews on Amazon as well as other places are hot topics lately. Who is allowed to leave a review, and even the validity of a review seem to be repeatedly coming under fire. While this is an interesting angle to the topic of reviews and we have discussed this topic in another chapter, we're going to discuss book blogger reviews in this chapter.

Book reviews are going to happen whether you seek them out or not. The book reviews you don't seek out are, for the most part, out of your control. Readers have obtained a copy of your book from somewhere and are sharing their thoughts with other readers on Amazon, Goodreads, blogs or other locations. The reviews we will talk about in this chapter are the ones you seek out. These are the reviews that result from you personally approaching book bloggers and asking them to review your book.

## Why do book bloggers post reviews?

Many book bloggers start their blogs to express their thoughts and maybe make some like-minded friends, just like I did. It never occurred to me that someone would actually read what I had to write. The reality is that book bloggers WANT to share their thoughts with others. WE LOVE BOOKS. We want to discuss what we loved about a particular book. There may not be anyone in our immediate neighborhood who loves the authors we do, but online, there are lots of people. I talk regularly with romance fans from literally all over the world.

## What does a review entail?

A book review generally takes about 6 to 8 hours of work for a full-length novel. From the initial e-mail conversation, to reading the book, to the creation of a well-thought out review, to posting and formatting the review on the blog; the process is a labor of love. I love losing myself in a book. Most book bloggers do. Some read faster than others, but generally, a book review is not a fast process. And really, do you want it to be a fast process?

- Do you want someone to rush through reading your book or do you want your book savored?
- Do you want someone to rush through the creation of a review of your book, or do you want a thoughtful review that encourages others to read your book?
- Do you want a review that is honest and gives the reader things to think about?
- Do you want a review that is helpful to you as the writer?

I would hope the above questions have you thinking about the review process and what the final outcome will look like.

## When a review is posted, what does it generally contain?

It is my opinion that authors need to think about what they want to see in a review before they approach book bloggers. Many of the commercial sites have guidelines about what must or may be present in a review. These guidelines are usually public. The same is true of many, but not all, book bloggers. On a book blog, these guidelines can be found in the form of an "About me" page, or the blogger may have a "Review Policy" page for you to see. Make sure you look for it!

Most book bloggers' reviews will contain some or all of the following:

- Title/author/publisher/ISBN/ASIN info
- Buy-links
- Blurb
- Cover art

- A summary with or without spoilers of the story line
- An analysis of the story — the book blogger's thoughts and opinions
- Links to the author in a variety of ways — blog and/or other social media sites
- A rating system that may be simple or very complex

As I've stated, as an author, you need to think about what you want to see in a review of your book. You also need to think about what you don't want to see in a review of your book.

Here's a list of things you may or may not have thought about:

- Do you need to know if the blogger will rate your book with stars/hearts/bunnies or other graphic rating system? Is this important to you? Do you want the blogger to talk about other aspects of the story in terms of a rating? For example, some bloggers will rate the heat of the story, the character development, the pace, and a handful of other aspects of the story, all using a graphic representation.
- Do you want the blogger to provide you with some quotable quotes — some concise comments you can include in a Facebook status, make part of a tweet, or include in the next edition of your book?
- Do you care if there are spoilers in the review?
- Do you care if the reviewer's grammar is poor, his sentence structure unbelievable, if he seems to be allergic to punctuation, but he has the potential to be a huge fan with a large following?
- Do you want someone who will post a negative review if she didn't like your book, or someone who will politely tell you that your book just wasn't for her?
- Lastly, do you want a book blogger who uses snarkiness or rudeness to attract attention to her blog and does that at your expense?

It is well known in the book blogging world that some bloggers go out of their way to create controversy. Let's face it: controversy attracts readers. The chatter starts on Facebook or Twitter. "Did you read what so and so said?" This attracts traffic in large numbers. Bloggers make a name for themselves, but do you want to be the target?

In my opinion, many authors in their rush to obtain the coveted review don't actually read the types of reviews the blogger posts. I've had authors complain that certain reviewers don't give books a rating out of 5. Many don't and likely state that in their review policy. Not to mention, likely none of their published reviews have ratings, if the author had only looked. There are places where reviewers do have to leave a number rating. Amazon, Goodreads and Barnes & Noble are just three examples that require a number rating.

I've read reviews that assign a number to every aspect of the story. To me, that seems like too much work! I've also seen reviewers who assign a letter grade from A to F and ones that will use part numbers, for example, rating a book 4.25/5.

To each his own. But again, we're back to the question of what do you want to walk away with from a review?

## When looking for a reviewer — what do you look for?

Have you actually sat down and made a list of things that are important to you in terms of a review? Let me help by offering this list of questions:

- Is a rating system of some sort important to you?
- How extensive do you want the system to be? Do you want to see ratings for various aspects of the story or just one rating?
- Do you want the book blogger to post his review to other places than his blog (i.e., Amazon, Goodreads, etc.)?
- Do you want to target a book blogger who seems to have a large following and therefore gives you lots of publicity?
- Do you want to target a book blogger who is very active on social media and has the ability to publicize her thoughts to a large audience?
- Do you want the book blogger to supply you with some quotable quotes?

## Authors = Rock Stars.

Thank bloggers for their reviews. If you request a review, please take the time to thank them for reading your book. Don't quibble with what they say; just thank them. More on this later.

As an author trying to promote your book, you have to ask yourself, what is the best vehicle for promotion of your book? Do you really think it's a review? Or is it better to get some commercial reviews and focus your promotional efforts on things like guest posts or interviews or giveaways, or some combination?

You might want to look at the time commitment. The time involved in obtaining a review is fairly minimal. Yes, you need to find some book bloggers and query them, but the rest of the work is done by the book blogger. A guest post or interview, on the other hand, is mostly your work, and minimal to the book blogger.

How much time do you have? Most authors write on a part-time basis and they have either a full or part-time job that requires their attention. I won't even start on the other things demanding time! If the most important thing to you is a review, then that needs to be at the top of your priority list. Keep in mind that there are other types of promotions you can ask for which might attract more traffic, and therefore attention to your book. We'll cover these in other chapters.

Many book bloggers are either closed to reviews or have a To Be Read (TBR) pile that results in a 3-to 4-month delay in reviews. Please don't make the assumption that book bloggers can review your book right away.

Some of us are better than others at saying no. At the time of writing this book, I have a TBR pile containing hundreds of books. Obviously, I have issues saying no. I'm currently closed to reviews, but I'm still a huge fan of certain authors. As a result, new books continue to come into the house, displacing ones on my TBR pile.

## Book bloggers are Uber-fans

This leads me to my next point. Book bloggers are uber-fans. Our favorite authors are like rock stars to us. Regardless of the size of the TBR pile, when our favorite author releases a new book, we are standing first in line to get a copy. Doesn't that encourage you to make friends with book bloggers? I have authors who are friends because of my contact with them. I have a handful of authors for whom I will drop everything to read their books. Regardless of the size of my TBR pile, these books become the next book I read. Is it fair? No, not really. But my blog is a hobby and I make the rules.

The last point I'll make on the subject of The Review is to remember to thank the book blogger for their time and their thoughts. There are a lot of authors who subscribe to the philosophy of having no contact with book bloggers who review their book. They don't believe in dropping by blogs to thank bloggers for taking the time to read their book and share their thoughts. I can remember the first time one of my favorite authors dropped by my blog to thank me for my review! I phoned everyone I knew to tell them and did a happy dance all over the house; I actually printed the comment and posted it on my wall. I still smile when I look at that comment. Receiving a comment from an author for reviewing a book is like getting front row tickets to a Queen concert . . . okay, maybe I'm dating myself . . . but this is a huge thrill to book bloggers.

For those of you who are picturing responding to the trolls who come out of their lair to verbally bash authors on Amazon, I'm not talking about those reviews. I'm talking about responding to the book bloggers who are normal functioning human beings and take some time out of their lives to read and help you promote your book. Leave the trolls and the cyber stalkers alone.

As we will talk about several times in this book, you should have a series of Google Alerts set up to notify you of action on the Internet about your book(s). There are many reasons for this, the most important being piracy, but it's so nice to have an author drop by your blog and say hi!

# CHAPTER EIGHT
# THE GUEST POST

## What is a guest post and how can it promote your book?

AS WE HAVE discussed before, book bloggers are the new slush pile. They are inundated with review requests. Their e-mail inboxes seem to magically fill up with e-mails from publishing houses, PR people, authors, and their assistants. Book blogging is a hobby, and while I personally feel it's the best hobby a person can have, it shouldn't take over one's life.

Some bloggers read faster than others, so posting four or five reviews a week is doable. Some blogs have multiple reviewers and they can post 10 or 15 reviews a week, as they post multiple times a day. We can assume most book bloggers post reviews because they want to share their love of books! But there are other ways to publicize your book.

In today's publishing environment, readers want to get to know authors. Well, we want to get to know the public persona of the author. We don't really want to know the day-to-day minutiae of the author's life, but we want to know what they are like as an author, what their interests are, how they research the books they write, and how they come up with ideas (especially totally non-creative people like myself). I'm continually fascinated by the over-used question of where do your ideas/inspiration come from? We want to know what books they've written, and what's coming up next. Many of us want to go to book signings or author chats. We want to be able to get a feel for their writing before we spend money on a book.

One way we can do this is by reading a guest post the author has written. Guest posts are a little window into the thoughts and ideas of an author. And to the addicted reader, they are a source of fascination and entertainment.

## So . . . what is a guest post?

Technically speaking, a guest post is 500 to 700 words written on a specific topic. The topic is chosen either by the author, by the blogger, or both. It's usually on a topic related to the book, but not necessarily about the book directly. It's an example of the author's writing and thoughts, without being the book itself.

## The more entertaining the guest post, the more attention it gets.

Some time ago I had a paranormal author write me a guest post on ghost sightings she had personally experienced. When I got the Word document from the author, I was a bit hesitant to post it. I write a romance blog and paranormal isn't my usual read. I decided this guest post wasn't really genre specific, as it was about events in the author's life and it was entertaining. I posted it. As you can guess, the hits were off the charts! I had people coming out of the woodwork to tell the author about their ghost sightings. I still get hits on this post and it was posted several years ago. Did this post talk directly about the author's book? No. It was entertaining, however! It attracted attention in droves! Because it attracted such attention, it is likely this author made some new fans.

More recently I've had an author write a post about the sad lack of dashing highwaymen in historical romance lately. (I certainly agree with her, by the way!) The hero of her latest release was a dashing highwayman. Again, a post that was entertaining to read, related to her book, and attracted attention in droves!

One last example of an entertaining guest post that got a fair amount of traction was the post by an author who had recently released a romance featuring a pirate. She wrote a post entitled "Pirates: The Ultimate Bad Boy." To date, this post has 99 comments. As an author and a blogger, you have to appreciate that kind of reaction to a post. Sadly, this guest post wasn't on my blog, but it was certainly an attention getter!

Speaking as a reader, I'm interested in what authors write. I live in awe of authors who create these magical worlds I escape into every day. I may be writing this, but I'm not capable of writing fiction! I'm too literal. Dialogue scares me. This brings us to the topic of what to write in a guest post.

How do you decide what to write about? In my experience, authors are much more creative than I am. I'm familiar with what topics work on my blog—which ones get the most reaction. In all truthfulness, the topics that did the best on my blog are the ones the author came up with.

Should the author or the blogger come up with the topic for a guest post? I think most bloggers know their audience best. They should know what will attract attention and what won't. I do, however, think the author needs to exercise their creative side and display this creativity to the readers. The readers want to read a little sample of the author's writing ability.

In terms of numbers, guest posts do far better on many blogs than review posts do. In terms of selling books, you want the attention, the numbers. You will likely get better numbers from a guest post, as long as it is interesting to your potential readers, than you will from a review. You want them to finish reading what you have written and say to themselves, "I want to try out this book!" and head off to Amazon or Barnes & Noble, credit card in hand.

## What does the author send to the book blogger for their post?

Now that we have covered what to say, or how to decide what to say in your guest post, we need to move to the next step: What do you send along to the blogger, other than your document with the guest post on it? Most book bloggers have a policy and will tell you what they want, but here is a general list of what to include with your guest post:

- Cover graphic: high resolution if possible
- All buy-links—shorten with bit.ly (or other trackable shortener) if you wish to track clicks
- All social media links
- Blog/website links
- Blurb
- An excerpt, if possible
- Author picture & bio

In fact, it's helpful for all authors to have a media page on their blog. You can label it whatever you want, but it should contain everything you want available to someone wanting to promote your book—high-resolution graphics, bio (short, medium, and long), blurbs, an excerpt—even a list of blogs that have recently featured you.

It makes sense to make every effort to provide everything necessary to post the guest post. I do understand that not everyone is clear in their requirements. Since the author is the one asking for a service, she should be making every effort to ensure she has provided everything necessary.

In my experience, many authors are not familiar with what a book blogger would want to put a post together. They're aware that they need to create a guest post and supply buy-links, but are unaware of why the rest of the list is important.

Let's take a quick look at the list above. Why would these various things be provided to the book blogger creating a post for her blog? The first reason is convenience. If you provide everything, the book blogger doesn't need to hunt for it. I certainly have gone hunting for links and gotten (and posted) wrong information. If you provide everything, you can be certain everything is correct.

It is my practice not to search for items that aren't included. I used to spend time searching out a Twitter handle, or grabbing cover graphics from Amazon. Book bloggers are not necessarily aware of changes in cover graphics or buy-links to error-ridden e-books that were mistakenly uploaded. Combine this with the fact that according to copyright law (in some countries), we need permission to use certain items, like long excerpts, in our posts. Taking all of this into account, please ensure you send everything required for your post so you make the best use of your promotional time.

The second reason to supply everything on this list goes back to creating a relationship with potential readers. Keep in mind that readers are a curious lot. They're interested in finding out about a new author. They may want to follow you on Facebook and keep up to date with what's going on in your world. They may want to visit your blog and find out more about you and your writing. You want readers to form some sort of relationship with you. This is part of your marketing job. It isn't your job, however, to determine how they're going to form that relationship. That is for the reader to decide. Your job is to provide links to everywhere you have a presence. You can certainly mention that you have a profile on numerous social media platforms but really only spend time on Facebook. You need to let the reader choose.

As far as timing is concerned, it's a good idea to get the information to the book blogger as soon as possible. Because a blog post can be set and scheduled in advance, the blogger can set up their post with time left over to request anything that might be missing. I like to set my posts two weeks in advance. Does this always happen? No! It's nice to aim for, though. I have a job, I have a family, and I can get sick. It's nice to have some breathing room to allow me to walk away from my blog for a while and know that everything is set and posts will continue to appear on time. This is especially nice in the winter when I can lose Internet access for periods of time because of the weather.

## You've sent the blogger all your information. Are you done?

So, you've gathered up all the information, written your guest post, and sent it along, with everything else required, to the book blogger. Now what are your responsibilities?

You are not finished! Nothing spurs comments faster than the author dropping by the blog first thing in the morning to say hi and mention they'll be dropping by periodically to answer questions. If the readers are assured their questions will be read and answered, many are eager to leave questions or comments. Does this guarantee comments? No. In my experience, I rarely get comments unless there's a question to be answered. I can look at my analytics and I know people have visited, but unless they have a question, they often say nothing. The other thing to keep in mind, not only when your book is being featured, but also in general when you're looking at blogs to make friends, there are statistics that state that somewhere between 1 and 10% of visitors to blogs leave a comment. Many people assume that blogs with a lot of comments are high-hit blogs. I don't think that's necessarily true. I think those are blogs with chatty followers in many cases.

Now that many book bloggers are part of a Triberr tribe, visitors could be coming to a blog days after the original post. For that reason, as well as many others, you should subscribe to the comments on any blog you appear on. This will allow you to be notified as soon as a comment is left on a blog. You don't have to keep checking.

The next thing you do is promote your stop on your social media channels. You post it to Facebook, you tweet about it, you share it on Google+, you even blog about it. You let your peeps know where you will be and invite them to visit and say hi.

You have taken the time and trouble to create a guest post to promote your book, so get as much mileage out of it as you possibly can! Likely the blogger will do some promotion, but you're responsible for doing your part. I post to quite a few blogs, including my personal one. The posts the author promotes on their social media get so much more traction than when they are promoted by just the book blogger alone.

As I have mentioned before, it's my theory that it takes a community to promote and market a book. I fondly refer to this activity as "Operation Book." Your community should be involved in every aspect of your marketing. Don't you think it's a good idea to let your author and reader friends know whom you're visiting? Isn't it good to make new friends? New friends often become new readers and paying customers. Likely your author friends can benefit from forming new friendships as well. Don't you think it's a good idea to let authors who write in the same genre as you know about your guest post? You've identified a "friendly"—someone who likes your genre. Just as the book blogger would appreciate finding a new author to read, your author friends would likely appreciate finding a new place to promote their books.

I'm going to remind you again at this point in your learning that you should have a Google Alert set up so you know when you or your book(s) are being talked about on a blog. Is this system 100% accurate? No. It is helpful in many ways, however. Google Alerts can let you know not only when your name or your book is mentioned; it can also help you discover when your book has been pirated.

You can make a book blogger's day by simply dropping by their blog and thanking them for reading or promoting your book. Do I suggest you respond to the trolls on Amazon? Again, NO! But remember, book selling is a relationship activity. Make some friends with blogs. They will help you promote your book!

# CHAPTER NINE
# THE INTERVIEW

WE HAVE TALKED about book bloggers and what a great resource they can be to your career as an author. We have spent some time talking about some of the features that can promote your book. Let's now move on to talk about The Interview.

An interview, in many respects, is an easy way to promote yourself and your book. You don't need to come up with a topic to write about; all you need to do is to answer questions about yourself.

Let's be clear what an interview with a book blogger is. Simply stated, it's a list of questions sent by e-mail. The author answers the questions and then e-mails them back. It isn't live and it doesn't require you to leave the house.

A blog interview is anywhere from six to 20 questions covering a wide range of topics. Some interviewers are serious and provide thoughtful, detailed questions. Some interviewers are irreverent, asking off-the-wall questions that some may find a bit off-putting. Many book bloggers are somewhere in the middle, asking a mixture of serious and fun questions. What bloggers are trying to do is to provide information about you to their readers—a little snapshot, if you will. It's your job to answer their questions in the best way you can.

A common complaint I hear from authors is that the questions are stupid or a waste of time. My response is that the authors need to take what they're given and form it into something they want to represent them and their books. If you are given five questions, feel free to make your answers more lengthy than if you are given twenty questions. The old expression—make lemonade out of lemons applies here.

Let's look at how to answer questions in the most advantageous manner possible.

A standard question in an interview is some version of, "Tell us a bit about yourself and your writing." You're visiting this blog to promote yourself and your book(s). You want to give as much information as you can about yourself and your book(s) without being overly long and detailed.

## Here is an example of a good answer:

Hi, everyone! I'm so happy to be visiting Sugarbeat's Books! My name is XXX and I have just released my first book, YYYY! I have been writing from an early age and spent many hours creating bedtime stories for my kids when they were young. I have been devoting myself to the craft of writing and learning as much as I can. I'm a lifelong reader of historical romances and have always been fascinated with the French Revolution. I have combined my fascination with that era and my love of Historical Romance and have created a story about a young Duc that escaped the mob's burning of the homes of the aristocracy to start again and find love in Regency England. I hope you will love Sarah and Gitane's story as much as I enjoyed writing it.

Let's analyze the answer above. I have offered a greeting to the readers of the blog (which I have named and spelled correctly) in a friendly fashion. I have not only introduced myself, but included the name of my book in the same sentence as my name. It's important to do this in case the book blogger hasn't provided an introduction to your interview. Readers are often curious about how you made the journey to published author, so it's nice to include a few sentences that summarize that information. Frankly, we don't really want to read a dissertation on your life history, just a few relevant points on your personal life up until this point. You'll notice I don't say that my new book, YYYY, is a historical romance set during the French Revolution. Instead, I describe the premise of the book and introduce you to the hero and heroine. This allows me to offer a short description of the story line and the main characters without using the blurb of the book.

When answering interview questions, you don't want to say too little and you don't want to say too much. I've have seen both. I have had authors answer that question with: "I have written for years. My first book has just been released." Not helpful. I have also had authors answer this question with a 500 word full biography complete with information on when and where they were married, the names and ages of their children, and all degrees acquired from various universities.

Let me remind you that as book bloggers, we and our readers want to learn more about you as an author. We want to have some sort of a connection with you. We don't really want to know the "real" you, just a version of your public persona. I don't want to hear about how long your labor was with your first child unless your book is about pregnancy and childbirth. I am, however, like many readers, curious about the short version of your journey to the world of publishing.

The question I gave above leaves you with some leeway to answer as you choose. You will also want to look over the collection of questions before you start answering so you don't repeat yourself in a future answer. As I mentioned above, a complaint I hear commonly from authors is that they feel the questions they have been given are silly and limiting. Questions such as:

Name:

Book title:

Genre:

Favorite Ice Cream:

Favorite TV Show:

My suggestion is to make the questions your own. Provide answers giving the information you want to give. See the following example:

Name: Hi There! My name is XXX. I'm a voracious reader, life-long writer, and I'm so happy to be visiting your blog today to talk about my newly released book, YYY, which is set in Regency England. YYY features a handsome duke as the dashing hero, who meets his match when he collides with Sarah on the dance floor.

You can see that the expected answer was probably simply the author's name. I expanded on this, sounding friendly and giving a few bits of information about myself as well as stating the name and some information about my book. You can answer the rest of these questions in a similar fashion, taking control of the question and answering with the information you want your audience to have.

As I stated at the beginning of this chapter, an interview post should end up being the length of a typical blog post (500-700 words). Feel free to break up those words amongst the questions. If you are provided with five questions, be more wordy than if you were provided with fifteen. Provide the information you want to get across in whatever fashion you can. Essentially answer the questions that aren't asked. If you have a final question like: "Is there anything else you would like to add?" I would suggest you provide all the information that you want to include but that didn't reasonably fit in the questions provided. Remember, you are providing these answers in writing, not verbally with no advanced warning of what the questions are. Take your time to write and re-write your answers to best portray information about yourself and your book(s).

Is the job complete when you have finished answering the questions? No, of course not. Make sure you send the questions along with the answers. You might find this an obvious point, but it isn't unusual for an author to send a word document with only answers and the book blogger is left trying to remember what questions were asked and fit them to the answers. As was mentioned in other chapters, you should also send along the following:

- Cover graphic—high resolution if possible
- Blurb
- Excerpt if possible
- Website/blog URL
- All social media links
- All buy-links
- Author picture & bio

## Now that you have sent the blogger your information, is your job done?

You should know by now that your job isn't done with the sending of your information. Remember, your information should be in the inbox of the blogger at least two weeks before your feature. On the day of, you'll want to drop by the blog and thank the blogger for hosting you. Mention you'll be dropping by to answer any questions periodically throughout the day. Ask the readers a question—that often spurs comments. As I've pointed out in other chapters, make sure you subscribe to comments if the option is available. This and a Smart-Phone will allow you to appear psychic, dropping over immediately to address questions or comments from readers mere minutes after they have been left!

In addition to visiting the blog, you need to promote your visit to the book blogger in as many ways as you can. Don't allow all your hard work to go to waste. Tweet the post, share it on Facebook, post it to LinkedIn, even blog about it. Share this on your author links, talk about what you're doing with your critique group. Invite your mother to visit and talk about what a cute baby you were . . . well . . . um . . . maybe not . . . she might have pictures.

Let's talk common sense here. Although I've mentioned this in previous chapters, it bears repeating. Your author friends likely write books in a similar genre to you. Do you think they would be interested in attracting new readers? Invite them to drop by the blog that is interviewing you and talk about the genre you all write in. Keep in mind it's considered rude to leave a comment like: "My name is Cathy and I love XXX's work. I also write historical romances and my books can be found on my blog (insert link) and on Amazon (insert link)." Many blogs now have the Hovercard function available and anyone can discover your blog by hovering over your avatar. Not familiar with this function? Drop by a Wordpress blog and hover over an avatar on a comment. See what happens. This is a great way of spreading the love. Not only are you bringing traffic to the book blogger's blog, but you are encouraging the readers to discover new authors to read—your friends!

## The Character Interview

I want to add a few words here about character interviews. These aren't nearly as common as regular interviews, but this is an option for authors. In the case of a character interview, usually the author will provide the questions and the answers. This interview is set up to seem like one of the characters from the featured book is being interviewed. When done well, this feature is outstanding and does a wonderful job of giving the potential reader a glimpse into the story you've written.

Although I've seen character interviews done very well, keep in mind, it is likely that no one reading the interview has read your book. Because of this, this type of interview is difficult to pull off. If this is something you are interested in doing, check with the book blogger and ask for their advice. Until you are practiced at this, make sure someone who is not familiar with your story can understand the interview.

# CHAPTER TEN
# THE GIVEAWAY

THE GIVEAWAY is always a popular attention getter for any stop on a blog. Even blogs that have a lot of natural traffic will get a boost with a giveaway added to the stop. Most people are willing to enter their name for free stuff. Just to be clear, a giveaway is where you offer up something—a copy of your book, a treat, some swag—and readers have to do something to be entered to win.

In this chapter we're going to talk about what a giveaway is, how it can work to an author's advantage, and hopefully point out a few things so an author can include a giveaway in a list of things they understand and can use to their advantage to promote their book.

Should a giveaway be the only thing happening on the blog? Should a giveaway be combined with another feature? Should the giveaway always be a book? What other options are there for giveaways? Let's discuss this so you understand what a giveaway is in all its various forms.

Should a giveaway be the only thing happening on the blog? My short answer is no! This isn't a raffle at a county fair that people enter and then forget about. The whole point of appearing on a book blog is to promote your book. If all you're doing is giving away a copy of your book, you aren't offering anything up about your book other than the title and maybe a blurb. You aren't giving readers a reason to learn more about your book if they don't win. You aren't giving new-to-you readers a reason to give your work a try. Keep in mind you want this to be more than a flash-in-the-pan-kind of promotion. A post on a book blog is there for the life of the blog. It's "out there" and will be visible potentially for years to come. You want this post to be searched on Google in the future, and although the giveaway portion is finished, there's still information that someone can read about you and your book. It gives someone a reason to read the post.

## Types of Giveaway Posts

### Book Blurb/Excerpt

I feel the Book Blurb/Excerpt feature is the easiest feature to combine with a giveaway. This type of feature (a.k.a., Book Spotlight, Book Blast, etc.) and it has other names) combines the blurb of your book, the cover graphics, and if possible, an excerpt. In my experience, readers love to read an excerpt of an author's work. It allows them to get a feel for the author's writing. The blurb will give the reader the basic story line, but the excerpt will add some dimension to the post. Pull a short section that you feel is a stand-alone read and a good representation of your writing and ask the readers questions. If your hero is a bad boy (the best kind, of course), include a question about the readers' feelings about your characters. Do they like stories with bad boys? This will give the readers a reason to read the excerpt, and again, if you drop by the blog in the morning and announce that you will be available to respond to questions, you might get quite an interesting dialogue going.

### Guest Post

If you want to put a bit more time and effort into the giveaway, combine it with some sort of guest post; some interesting facts you came across in the research for your book would add some dimension to the post. Remember, guest posts should not be long-winded. You can tie an excerpt into a guest post—perhaps as an example of what you are writing about in your guest post. For more details on guest posts, please see Chapter 8.

### Interview

The third common option is an interview. It can be a regular interview or character interview. An interview is always popular. I often get people commenting on something new that they learned about the author. People look for bonds or points of commonality. The fact that you have a cat or a dog, for example, will be very important to many readers. For more details on interviews, please see Chapter 9.

# The Giveaway Prize

The next question is what to give away. The immediate response of many authors is to offer a copy of the book. Let's talk about the logistics of giving away a book. Let's say you want to give away an autographed paper copy of your book because you have heard this is popular. In my experience, autographed paperbacks or hardcovers are keepsakes that people enjoy getting. Have you given any thought as to how you're going to get that book to the winner? To mail a book within the U.S. is a rather simple and cheap activity, but what if your winner lives in the Orient, or some other overseas location? Have you looked at the postal rates? I know the readers of my blog live all over the world. Are you prepared to mail a book to the winner wherever they live, or do you want to limit the giveaway so the winner has to live in the same country as you? Would geographically limiting a giveaway offend some readers? It is my experience that it can easily offend! I live in Canada and I can't count the number of giveaways I've been excluded from.

Your next option is to offer up an electronic copy of your book. You don't have to pay postage and the giveaway wouldn't be restricted due to costs. E-books are easily e-mailed anywhere in seconds. There are certainly lots of people with e-readers, but I know that not everyone knows how to convert a file so it looks nice on their e-reader. Frankly, do you want a review to appear on Amazon that says, "The story was great, but the weird formatting drove me up the wall!" Admittedly, many people who enter my giveaways are book bloggers who are capable of adjusting the file type to what they want and will happily overlook formatting issues for the sake of a free book that they want to read! This is something to think about, however.

The giveaway need not be limited to books. I like giving away a selection of chocolate. I find that it's popular, but again, it has to be mailed, so geography should be taken into account. The other thing that is usually popular is what we refer to as "swag." This general description will run the range of signed book cover samples for a yet to be released book, to bookmarks, trading cards, cool jewelry—the list can go on and on! I've even received a branded blow-up beach ball for a summer chick-lit book. Overall, I'm a fan of bookmarks, as I don't like to dog-ear pages. If this is something you're interested in doing, most book bloggers will be able to tell you what they have found to be popular on their site. There are also quite a few online sites that can produce some inexpensive swag for you.

## How do you want to collect names for the giveaway?

We should also discuss the logistics of the giveaway. Although I'm a fan of readers filling in a Google form embedded in my site, book bloggers have different things they like to do to qualify winners. They may ask readers to follow you on various social media platforms, maybe even offering up extra entries for people who do. They may request readers answer a question or leave a thoughtful question for you to answer. They may use Rafflecopter to control the entries of the giveaway. Do you care? Should you ask how the blogger is going to hold the giveaway? Whose job is it to follow up on contacting the winner? How long does the giveaway go on? These are questions you might want to ask.

Are there people who enter giveaways just for the sake of entering a giveaway? Sure. As I mentioned above, some bloggers will require the reader to do more than just leave a comment to be entered – for example, they may ask readers to leave a question for you to answer. A giveaway structured this way could have you responding to questions and comments on a busy blog for a week or more—do you want to do that? How long does the giveaway go on? I'd suggest no longer than a week. That should be sufficient time for news of the giveaway to work its way through the various social media and get a good number of entries. Is this something you have an opinion on? Do you care, or do you just go along with whatever the book blogger has planned?

Are you prepared to be in charge of delivering the prize to the winner? From my experience, there is nothing better than receiving a little note and a book or some chocolate from one of my favorite authors. Remember, authors are rock stars to most book bloggers and readers. This could be a relationship moment—a chance to leave a favorable impression on a new reader. If you have the choice, I'd suggest you offer to deliver the prize to the winner along with a little note of thanks!

The information we have covered on giveaways will give you a lot to think about. Give yourself some time to think about what your preferences are for a giveaway—things you feel strongly about, and things you don't really care one way or another about. Wander through some book blogs. This might give you an idea of the variety that exists as well as some new ideas that I haven't covered here.

The goal of a giveaway, like any feature on a blog, is to network.

As you have read, there are many aspects of a giveaway you may not have thought about before. If this is something you are going to do, I suggest sitting down and listing some goals first. If a goal is to meet some readers in other countries, geographically limiting the giveaway might have the opposite result. Don't be afraid to ask questions. Most experienced bloggers host giveaways all the time. They will be happy to answer any questions you might have.

# CHAPTER ELEVEN
# THE BLURB/EXCERPT

OF ALL THE various promotional features that can be done on most book blogs, the Blurb/Excerpt and the Cover Reveal Features are probably the simplest but are very effective.

The Blurb/Excerpt feature (which can be called several different names) involves sending the book blogger your cover graphic, book blurb, a choice excerpt, your social media contact points, and the buy-links you want included. You may or may not include your bio and author picture. This is a quick and easy way to promote your book. You just need to put all this information into an e-mail and the blogger will put together the post.

The blurb gives the potential reader a quick peek at the story line. Many readers will decide if they want to read the book solely from the blurb of the book. For those of us who are very visual, the cover art is a must. I often decide whether or not to read a book from the cover art alone. Of course, since I'm a huge fan of historical romance, there's nothing like a woman in a beautiful ball gown or a mostly naked man in a kilt to convince me that a particular book must be a great read!

As I've pointed out in other chapters, an excerpt is a huge selling feature—be it as part of a blog post or as something offered on Amazon or Barnes & Noble. Readers want to take a test drive, so to speak. They want to get a taste not only for the story, but your writing style. Some readers are easy-going and can adapt to any storytelling style, but some are very particular. The excerpt is a good idea for both types of readers. The easy-going reader will get a quick look at the story and the pickier reader can get to see if your writing style will work for them.

Make sure that whatever you send, you remember to include your social media contact points and all the buy-links you want included. It's important for people to be able to buy a copy of your book if they're interested in it, and it's almost more important for potential readers to be able to contact you on your blog and/or hook up with you on Facebook or other social media platforms and learn more about you.

## The Cover Reveal

The Cover Reveal is a common way for you to start creating hype about your new release. Book bloggers are generally receptive to posting your cover as soon as you have it. Even without a blurb and excerpt, a cover will get people talking about your new book. Just send along your social media contact points to include in the post and you're set to create a buzz and allow people to contact you if they have more questions. I do realize that many authors don't have a lot of control over their cover art, and just as many don't receive their art much in advance of the release of their book.

The Cover Reveal is something you can keep in the back of your mind to do on your second book. Contact all the bloggers who reviewed your first book and ask them if they want to promote your new book with a cover reveal. I think you would be surprised how many will say yes.

A word of caution about doing mass Cover Reveals that either you arrange or hire a blog tour company/PR person to do for you. Wordpress (and some other blogging platforms) have very specific rules about original content and advertising. A blog that only posts content they receive from others (i.e., a blog tour company) is in danger of going against the Terms of Service. As one Happiness Engineer (as the people from the help desk at Wordpress.com are called) from the Wordpress forum recently stated:

We do expect all of our users to create original content on their sites and to comply with copyright laws. However, fair-use excerpts of content published elsewhere, particularly in the context of a review, is generally considered to be acceptable both from copyright standards and our Terms of Service.

If the bloggers are posting their own, or a guest blogger's, content to their own blog, that's fine. If there are a number of bloggers all posting the exact same pre-written content to their blogs, however, that may be considered spam or advertising.

For an excellent article on this subject, visit Parajunkee's blog: http://www.parajunkee.com/2014/07/31/book-blogging-101-word-press-thinks-book-tours-are-spamadvertising/

If you are interested in the rules for Wordpress.com, please find the Wordpress Terms of Service (TOS) here (https:// en.wordpress. com/tos/) and comments about allowed blog types here (http:// wordpress.com/types-of-blogs/).

# CHAPTER TWELVE
# THE BLOG TOUR COMPANY

IN THIS CHAPTER we're going to talk about what a blog tour is and how to find the right blog tour company for you and your book. We'll also talk about what a blog tour can do for you.

A blog tour is exactly what its name suggests. Like a multi-country tour of Europe, a blog tour will take you on a journey to a selection of blogs so you can talk about your book. Some blog tours are short, some are long, some involve guest posts and other book features, and some involve reviews. A blog tour is a lot of work and I don't feel it's something authors should be organizing themselves. They should be writing. That being said, there are a lot of authors who successfully organize their own blog tours. Before you try to plan your own tour, do your research. A professional blog tour doesn't have to be overly expensive and it is something you can hire someone to organize for you. Remember . . . you are supposed to be writing! But please do your research. It's your hard-earned money you are spending. Make sure you will get value for your money.

I find a lot of authors sign up with a blog tour company without clear goals in mind. What do you want to get out of a blog tour? If your only goal is to sell books, keep in mind that selling books is a relationship-centered activity. Readers rely on recommendations from a trusted source when deciding whether or not to buy a book, not a billboard along the highway. Advertisements in magazines and other places may get an author's name "out there" but often it's your best friend saying, "You have to read this book," to get you to buy. Will you sell books from doing a blog tour? Maybe some, but the main point of a blog tour is to meet and greet. Think of a blog tour as similar to doing a book signing at your local bookstore. Do you sell books at those events? Yes, some. But you schmooze, you make friends, you talk about your book, you win over readers. The same thing should be true of a blog tour. But ultimately:

## Book Blog Tours DO NOT sell books!

So again, what are your goals in doing a blog tour? Is it to get more reviews? Is it to get your book cover and your name in front of as many sets of eyes as you can? Many tour companies require the author to provide giveaways for the tour. Is that something you're interested in doing? See Chapter 10 on giveaways to provide you with more information.

I'm going to make the assumption that you will hire a tour company to do your blog tour. I suggest you start by asking your author friends for recommendations. What companies have they used, what did they like, what did they not like? Listen to their answers. What one person finds important is not necessarily what others find important. Write down their suggestions and go to each company's website individually.

Most blog tour companies have clearly laid-out sites. They have a list of tours with associated prices. They usually advertise current, future, and past tours, and they frequently have a list of blog tour hosts.

For the most part, prices are competitive, with the old saying, "You get what you pay for" being true. If you're paying $10.00 for a 10 stop tour, don't expect much. The reputable sites will charge a reasonable fee for their organizational skills, and the production of tour graphics. They should be serving as the middle-man gathering up all the information needed from you and dispersing it to the book bloggers. You shouldn't have to be fielding many e-mails if you hire a company—remember, you're supposed to be writing, not answering e-mails.

I'd suggest going through the current and past tours and wandering through the list of tour hosts. Let's start with the tour hosts. Click on some links and look at a selection of the blogs. You are looking at each blog to see if it's somewhere you would want you and your book to be represented. Does it look like it is posted to on a regular basis? Are the posts neat and well-organized? If this blog posts reviews, read a few. Are they being respectful to authors in their reviews? Can readers leave comments easily? Take a look at some of the current and past tours. Look at the blogs that were/are used on the tour. Are they a good fit for the genre of book being toured? Are the posts well put together and organized? Are links in place in order to buy a copy of the book as well as to get in touch with the author? You might even want to look at Twitter streams and Facebook pages to see if the stop was advertised by the book blogger and by the tour company. This is your hard-earned money you're spending. You want to make sure you spend it as wisely as possible. You might even want to consider looking at the blogs' Alexa ranking and maybe even do a Google search to see where some posts are placed. If you're going to go to the trouble of writing guest posts, you want to make sure they can be found long after the day of promotion.

If your goal for a blog tour is to get more reviews, look at one or more of the company's review tours. Read the reviews that have been posted. Are they the type of reviews you want for your book? Do you want reviews posted on Amazon or Goodreads? Don't automatically assume that that's part of the package—ask.

From my point of view, your goals in doing a blog tour should be to get your name and the information about your book out there and to make some friends. The more you focus on those goals, the more books you'll sell. Ultimately, however, you need to shop for a blog tour with an informed point of view and do what you feel is in your best interests.

# CHAPTER THIRTEEN
# HOW DO YOU PROMOTE YOUR STOP ON A
# BOOK BLOG?

THE PURPOSE OF this chapter is to summarize the steps you can take to promote your stop on a blog. Writing up guest posts, generating thoughtful answers to interview questions, or even combining an e-mail with all the information needed for a blurb/excerpt feature is time consuming. As I've said before, you want to make sure you get the most "bang for your buck"!

## Promotion is a group activity! You want to get as many people involved as you can.

- Make sure you get all the materials for the post to the book blogger well in advance. Be certain to include all your social media links and all buy-links for the blogger to incorporate into his post.
- Send an e-mail around to your author groups, your critique partners, even your mother to let them know about your upcoming promotion and then send a note of reminder a day or so in advance. Even if none of your friends do this, set an example of how this promotion thing is done.
- Post something on your blog about your stop, complete with a link to the book blogger's site. If this stop is part of a blog tour, you can put a schedule on your sidebar that links to your post with more details.
- If you can, schedule some tweets ahead of time to let your friends know where you'll be.
- Drop by the blog first thing in the morning to confirm the post is live and that you have the correct link. Leave a comment of thanks for the blogger and a few words about your book. Let

everyone know you'll be back to answer any questions or address any comments periodically throughout the day. Before you post the comment, check to see if you can subscribe to comments. This little function will allow you to be notified when there are new comments posted to the blog. Sometimes the blogger will let you know when there are comments, but you should do your best to be autonomous.

• Post something on your Facebook page reminding everyone to drop by and meet a new book blogger and to say hi. Remember, authors who write the same genre as you should always be looking for new friends, especially friends with blogs because friends will be willing to go the extra mile to help with promotion.

• Post an announcement or two on Twitter to encourage your twitter followers to head over to the blog and say hi. If you have your blog feed connected to your Goodreads author page and your Amazon Author page, anyone who is a fan of yours on Goodreads will be notified of the stop, and people who find you when shopping on Amazon can find out about your stop on the book blogger's blog.

• I'd encourage you to send around an invitation to a Goodreads event, but my tolerance for those has waned and I'm starting to see them as spam.

• Make sure you follow, like, and circle the book blogger on Twitter, Facebook, and Google+ so you can retweet (RT) her tweets, share their posts on Facebook, and comment on her Google+ share.

• The last item on my list is to at some point stop by the blog and use all those little Share buttons. They are important. Almost 30% of my hits now come from Stumbleupon, and frankly, I don't spend much time there. Those little buttons are like the vegetables your mother tried to get you to eat—just close your eyes and get it done.

Here's something for you to think about. I manage quite a few blogs. My blogs have counters on the share buttons so I know how many shares have taken place. I am aware of the number of posts that only have one share for each platform—mine. Does that mean authors don't understand how important those share buttons are, or that they just couldn't be bothered? I like to think that authors simply don't understand the importance of these various little things. It does, however show that there is a lot of room for improvement!

# CONCLUDING THOUGHTS

I THOUGHT I'D let the book bloggers conclude this book for me. I originally created this book on the basis of survey results from 215 book bloggers. They shared quite a bit of valuable advice. I now have the results of this study posted on my blog (http://bakerview-consulting.com/?p=2435). The one part of the survey I am keeping in this edition of the book is this collection of answers to the last question I asked. I hope you enjoy their answers as much as I did! Each one is a little pearl of wisdom from someone who loves books and wants to help you.

## If you could give authors one piece of advice about promoting their books, what would it be?

- Don't harass the bloggers. We do this for fun and most don't make any money doing it. If you e-mail over and over, you are taking away from our time to possibly read your book! If a reviewer says no, there's no sense in continuing to convince him—there's a reason he said no!
- Don't attack reviewers who don't like it! I've picked up many books based on negative reviews, so they are useful when done right.
- Edit, edit, edit. Write the best blurb you can.
- Don't be pushy.
- Look for blogs that review your genre. Target--don't wallpaper the blogs. Hire a good tour company if you can.
- Stay out of the drama!
- Don't send a review request a hundred times to the same blogger. And don't send the same review request to every blogger. It's like applying for a job—you change the cover letter for each specific application. If I see you sent me a generic request five times I probably won't answer.
- Talk to us like we're human. Read our review policies,

and make sure your book fits. Include our names in your review request.

- Look at the bloggers' preferred reading and only ask for promotion if the blogger loves the type of book you write.

- Take the time to see what I've read and enjoyed. If it's obvious I dislike a certain genre and that's the genre of your book, it just makes me feel like you didn't take the time to look at my blog, so why should I take the time to read your book?

- Don't push your book down someone's throat. If the only thing you talk about on social media is you or your book, most people will take a detour.

- Make sure you show all the important information clearly—release date, purchase links, where to contact you, Twitter/blog links, etc.

- Promoting in general—try as many different venues as you can, especially if you don't have much of a platform: get a Facebook page, Twitter account, and promote from all of those because even people who don't have Goodreads will look at a Twitter account or some other social media site.

- On blogs specifically—READ THE REVIEW POLICY PAGE. I think that is probably the single most important thing, because if your book is historical fiction and a blogger prefers fantasy, even if he takes it, he might not give it as many stars as a history buff would have.

- Use bloggers, social media, and any type of *free* advertising you can get your hands on. Free e-book days are even better! Get your book out there by giving people the chance to read your book for free. Even if they don't like your book, it is still exposure!

- I will go the extra mile to help promote authors who are polite and personable, if I love their book. Find bloggers who love your book and they will go above and beyond to help. Also keep excerpts and guest posts short. I tend to skim right over the long ones—don't have time to read it all.

- Don't be afraid to ask book bloggers for help. I mean, we do love to read. Personally, I love getting new opportunities to do new things for my blog.

- Be proud of your book. Don't play it down or apologize for anything in your book/story.

- Make bloggers WANT to help you. Connect with them,

but take them seriously, too. Many bloggers keep tight schedules but are willing to bend for an author or book that appeals to them.

- Be patient and polite. TBR lists are long and if the reviewer is worth her salt, she will get to you. There is a difference between asking wait time and harassing the reviewer.
- When someone does something to help, make sure to thank them. Try to plug every social media outlet you can with your book/books.
- Be clear whom your target audience is. Not every book is for everyone. You could have a real gem with the right audience.
- Always be prepared and on time.
- Interesting guest posts spark readers' interest!
- Don't use Twitter and Facebook just for promotion —I love interacting with the authors and getting to know them.
- Make your promotion fit my blog.

**Please note**: To see the original survey results, click HERE (http://bakerviewconsulting.com/?p=2435) The most recent survey has over 500 such pieces of information as I asked the same questions again. These results I published under the title of Top Advice for Authors Promoting Their Book. Available on all retailers.

\* \* \*

I hope that you have learned a few things as you made your way though this book. As I said at the beginning, I believe that book bloggers are a great free source of promotion for your books. We are voracious readers who love telling the world about great books. Take what you have learned and stride confidently into the world of Book Blogging!

Don't hesitate to contact me with any questions you might have! My contact points are found below. Follow any of my blogs, wave at me on Twitter, or share a cute kitty or puppy picture with me on Facebook. My favorite thing in the world is chatting about books!

## Your Helpful Hints Are Waiting...

Interested in getting some helpful hints and some helpful videos to your inbox. Hints that are directly applicable to what you do? Click here (http://bakerviewconsulting.com/helpful-hints-waiting/) to get started!

# About The Author

Social Media and Wordpress Consultant Barb Drozdowich has taught in colleges, universities and in the banking industry. More recently, she brings her 15+ years of teaching experience and a deep love of books to help authors develop the social media platform needed to succeed in today's fast evolving publishing world. She delights in taking technical subjects and making them understandable by the average person. She owns Bakerview Consulting and manages the popular blog, Sugarbeat's Books, where she talks about Romance novels.

She is the author of 9 books, over 30 YouTube videos and an online WordPress course, all focused on helping authors and bloggers. Barb lives in the mountains of British Columbia with her family.

Barb can be found:
Author Website: http://barbdrozdowich.com
Business Blog: http://bakerviewconsulting.com
Facebook Author Page: http://bit.ly/1XYKxyQ
Twitter: http://bit.ly/1U5PxMr
Google+: http://bit.ly/1XYKzGQ
Pinterest: http://bit.ly/1skDog8
Goodreads: http://bit.ly/1qVii6L
YouTube Channel: http://bit.ly/25uvqCQ
Tech Hints Newsletter: http://eepurl.com/DfCRj
Amazon Author Page: http://amzn.to/1TGSAuL
Newsletter link - http://bit.ly/1UmP231

# ALSO BY BARB DROZDOWICH

**Top Advice for Authors Promoting Their Book: From a survey of 500+ book bloggers**

As the old saying goes: "Get the truth right from the horse's mouth." In a recent survey of over 500 book bloggers and other bloggers who feature books, the question was asked: "If you could give an author one piece of advice about promoting their book, what would it be?" As you can well imagine if you asked 500+ people the same question, you would get a variety of responses, but you would also see repeats of areas of importance or of commonality. Get some ideas from the people who live to talk about books.

*Top Advice for Authors Promoting Their Book* is only available in e-format from your favorite retailer.

\* \* \*

**The Author's Platform: The Beginner's Guide**

This book is aimed at authors who are new to the online aspect of book promotion and marketing. *The Author's Platform* clearly and simply explains all the various parts of an author's platform; what they are and what to do with them. This book uses simple, straightforward language. It helps beginner authors take a confident step into a world that is unfamiliar to them.

*The Author's Platform* is available at your favorite online retailer and the paperback copy can be ordered from your favorite bookstore.

\* \* \*

**Book Blog Tours: An Essential Marketing Tool for Authors**

The world of *Book Blog Tours* is another world that many authors are unfamiliar with prior to publishing a book. This world has it's own language and norms. And this world is surrounded by mis-information and mis-understandings. *Book Blog Tours* is meant to demystify this world - serve as a primer to authors about to enter this world. *Book Blog Tours* explains all aspects of blog tours carried out by a company and provides enough guidance to an author interested in creating their own tour.

*Book Blog Tours* is available at your favorite online retailer and the paperback copy can be ordered from your favorite bookstore.

* * *

*Keep your eyes peeled for a box set or two coming your way shortly as well as some new subjects to help authors and bloggers understand the technology that they need to work with.*

Made in the USA
Charleston, SC
22 October 2016